Tree Frog

by Dee Phillips

Consultants:

Kristina Cohen
Department of Biology, Boston University, Boston, Massachusetts

Kimberly Brenneman, PhD
National Institute for Early Education Research, Rutgers University, New Brunswick, New Jersey

BEARPORT
PUBLISHING

New York, New York

Credits

Cover © Aleksey Stemmer/Shutterstock; 2–3, © Sascha Burkard/Shutterstock; 4, © Joel Sartore/Alamy; 5, © Aleksey Stemmer/Shutterstock; 6, © Ingo Arndt/Minden Pictures/FLPA; 7, © Piotr Naskrecki/Minden Pictures/FLPA; 8, © Dale Mitchell/Shutterstock; 9, © Aleksey Stemmer/Shutterstock; 10, © Piotr Naskrecki/Minden Pictures/FLPA; 11, © Matthew W. Keefe/Shutterstock; 12T, © Eduardo Rivero/Shutterstock; 12B, © Minden Pictures/Superstock; 13, © Tips Images/Superstock; 14, © Peter Wilson/FLPA; 15, © Minden Pictures/Superstock; 16, © Christian Ziegler/Minden Pictures/FLPA; 16–17, 18, © Michael & Patricia Fogden/Minden Pictures/FLPA; 19, © Genevieve Vallee/Alamy; 20, © David Kuhn/Dwight Kuhn Photography; 21, © Brandon Alms/Shutterstock; 22L, © Sascha Burkard/Shutterstock; 22TL, © Thomas Marent/Ardea; 22TR, © David McKee/Shutterstock; 22BL, © Juan-Carlos Munoz/Biosphoto/FLPA; 22BR, © Konrad Wothe/Minden Pictures/FLPA; 23TL, © Christian Ziegler/Minden Pictures/FLPA; 23TC, © Sean van Tonder/Shutterstock; 23TR, © Joel Sartore/Alamy; 23BL, © Peter Reijners/Shutterstock; 23BC, © Minden Pictures/Superstock; 23BR, © Ralph Loesche/Shutterstock; 24, © Thomas Marent/Ardea, © David McKee/Shutterstock, © Juan-Carlos Munoz/Biosphoto/FLPA, and © Konrad Wothe/Minden Pictures/FLPA.

Publisher: Kenn Goin
Creative Director: Spencer Brinker
Design: Emma Randall
Editor: Mark J. Sachner
Photo Researcher: Ruby Tuesday Books Ltd

Library of Congress Cataloging-in-Publication Data

Phillips, Dee, 1967–
  Tree frog / By Dee Phillips.
    p. cm. — (Treed: animal life in the trees)
  Includes bibliographical references and index.
  ISBN-13: 978-1-61772-915-7 (library binding) — ISBN-10: 1-61772-915-9 (library binding)
  1. Red-eyed treefrog—Juvenile literature. I. Title.
  QL668.E24P45 2014
  597.8'78—dc23
                      2013011499

33614059714872

For more information, write to Bearport Publishing Company, Inc., 45 West 21st Street, Suite 3B, New York, New York 10010. Printed in the United States of America.

10 9 8 7 6 5 4 3 2 1

Contents

Hiding in the Leaves

High in a **rain forest** tree, a tiny creature rests on a leaf.

Its body blends in with the tree's green leaves.

Suddenly, the creature opens its huge red eyes and stretches its legs.

The colorful animal is a red-eyed tree frog, and it is ready to go hunting.

red-eyed tree frog

There are about 4,800 different kinds of frogs. Some live in trees, while others live on the ground near ponds and lakes.

red-eyed tree frog

Look at the tree frog on this page. List all the different colors you can see on the frog's body.

Colorful Tree Frogs

A tree frog is a type of frog that makes its home in trees.

There are hundreds of kinds of tree frogs, some of which have colorful skin.

For example, the red-eyed tree frog has a green body and red eyes.

It also has blue legs, yellow stripes on its sides, and orange feet.

a red-eyed tree frog's foot

suckers

A red-eyed tree frog has cup-shaped suckers on its feet. The suckers help the frog hold on to wet, slippery leaves.

Pick up three quarters and feel how much they weigh. An adult red-eyed tree frog weighs about the same amount.

blue legs

yellow stripes

orange feet

Life in the Trees

Red-eyed tree frogs live mainly in rain forests in Central America.

During the day, they rest on leaves.

At night, they wake up and climb through the trees to hunt for food.

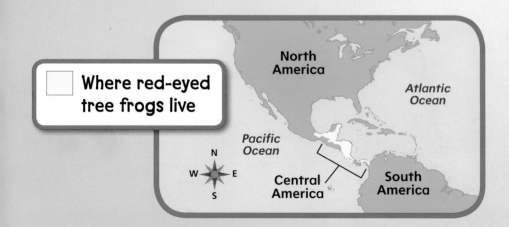

Where red-eyed tree frogs live

North America

Atlantic Ocean

Pacific Ocean

Central America

South America

N W E S

rain forest

Tree frogs hunt at night so their skin does not get dried out by the hot sun.

9

A Tiny Hunter

A red-eyed tree frog hunts mostly **insects**.

Once the frog spots its **prey**, it stays very still.

Its green skin helps it blend into the leaves of rain forest trees.

As a result, the insect often doesn't see the frog until it's too late.

Then the frog quickly grabs the insect with its mouth.

Red-Eyed Tree Frog Food

moth

cricket

fly

Red-eyed tree frogs eat insects such as moths, crickets, and flies. They also eat other smaller frogs.

A tree frog's color helps it hide from the animals it hunts. In what other way does the frog's color help it?

Staying Safe

Tree frogs don't just use their green color to stay hidden while hunting.

They also use their color to hide from **predators**.

Many kinds of animals eat red-eyed tree frogs.

To protect themselves, the frogs rest on green leaves that match the color of their skin.

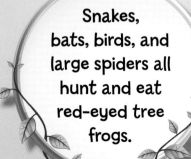

Snakes, bats, birds, and large spiders all hunt and eat red-eyed tree frogs.

Tree Frog Predators

toucan

snake

Tree Frog Eggs

When it's time to **mate**, male red-eyed tree frogs call to female frogs.

They do this by making loud croaking noises.

After the male and female come together, they mate on a leaf above a pond.

There the female lays up to 60 tiny eggs.

red-eyed tree frog eggs on a leaf

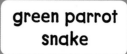
green parrot snake

frog eggs

A female red-eyed tree frog doesn't take care of her eggs or babies. Sometimes, predators such as snakes eat the eggs.

Time to Hatch

Growing inside each egg is a tiny baby frog called a tadpole.

After about six days, the tadpoles **hatch** from their eggs.

The baby frogs slide off the leaf and drop into the pond below.

tadpole about to drop into a pond

tree frog tadpoles

Fish and young dragonflies often feed on red-eyed tree frog tadpoles that are swimming in ponds.

How is a tadpole different from an adult tree frog? How is it the same?

Growing and Changing

Tree frog tadpoles have large heads, long tails, and no legs.

After a few weeks, the tadpoles grow legs.

Then their tails get shorter and shorter until they disappear.

Eventually, the tadpoles become small brown or green frogs called froglets.

tadpole changing into a froglet

tail

To help red-eyed tree frog tadpoles breathe underwater, they have body parts called gills. Once they leave the water as froglets, they use lungs to breathe air.

Where do you think the froglets will live?

froglet

Into the Trees

After tadpoles become froglets, they climb out of the pond and up into the trees.

Each little froglet is less than an inch (2.5 cm) long.

During their first year, the froglets will grow bigger and more colorful.

By the time they are two years old, they will be fully grown adults.

Then they will be ready to mate and have tadpoles of their own!

froglet climbing into a tree

Red-eyed tree frogs are named for their big, red eyes. Try to come up with a different name that describes how the frog looks.

Frogs belong to a group of animals called amphibians (am-FIB-ee-uhnz). Toads and newts are also amphibians. Most amphibians begin their lives in water but live on land as adults.

Science Lab

Animal Hide-and-Seek

A red-eyed tree frog's green skin helps it hide from predators. Other animals have bodies that help them hide from their enemies, too.

Try to spot the animal hiding in each of these four pictures. See if you can find a bird, an insect, a lizard, and a seahorse.

(The answers are on page 24.)

Science Words

hatch (HACH) to break out of an egg

insects (IN-sekts) small animals that have six legs, three main body parts, two antennae, and a hard covering called an exoskeleton

mate (MAYT) to come together in order to have young

predators (PRED-uh-turz) animals that hunt and eat other animals

prey (PRAY) animals hunted by other animals

rain forest (RAYN FOR-ist) a place where many trees and other plants grow and lots of rain falls

Index

Read More

Carney, Elizabeth. *Frogs!* Washington, DC: National Geographic (2009).

Lawrence, Ellen. *A Frog's Life (Animal Diaries: Life Cycles).* New York: Bearport (2012).

Lunis, Natalie. *Green Tree Frogs: Colorful Hiders (Disappearing Acts).* New York: Bearport (2010).

Learn More Online

To learn more about tree frogs, visit **www.bearportpublishing.com/Treed**

About the Author

Dee Phillips lives near the ocean on the southwest coast of England. She develops and writes nonfiction and fiction books for children of all ages. Dee's biggest ambition is to one day walk the entire coastline of Britain—it will take about ten months!

Answers for Page 22

1) A lizard called a leaf-tailed gecko

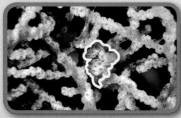

2) A fish called a pygmy seahorse

3) A bird called a spotted flycatcher

4) An insect called a walking stick